DATE DUE		
FEB 28 1986		
AP 15 '88		
MY 12 '89		
JA 18 '93		
JA 25 '93		
FE 01 '95		
FE 13 '95		
NOV 25 97		

A New True Book

FARMING

By Dennis B. Fradin

This "true book" was prepared
under the direction of
Illa Podendorf,
formerly with the Laboratory School,
University of Chicago

 CHILDRENS PRESS, CHICAGO

Tomato plants with a scarecrow

PHOTO CREDITS

James M. Mejuto—2, 4, 13 (right), 41 (left)
Wayne A. Bladholm—7, 13 (left), 19, 27 (right), 29
Historical Picture Services, Inc.—9
A. R. Robinson—10
Don and Pat Valenti—11 (left)
Soil Conservation Service: Don C. Schuhart—11
                                        (right); Gene Alexander—
                                        34 (top)
Reinhard Brucker—12, 34 (bottom)
Jerome Wyckoff—14 (top)
Earth Scenes: Dr. Nigel Smith—14 (bottom)
Joseph A. DiChello, Jr.—17, 20 (left), 45
Hillstrom Stock Photos: © W.S. Nawrocki Stock
                                    photos—Jeff Apoian—20
                                    (right), 38 (bottom), 41 (right)
Root Resources: © Ted Farrington—22 (top);
                              © W. Hessel—31; © Jack
                              Monsarratt—32 (top), 38 (top);
                              © Mary A. Root—32 (bottom left and
                              right); © Ruth Welty—36, 40
Joseph Antos—22 (bottom), 24
Jerry Hennen—Cover, 27 (left)
A. Kerstitch—42
COVER—Plowing

For Clarence Hill

Library of Congress Cataloging in Publication Data

Fradin, Dennis B.
   Farming.

   (A New true book)
   Includes index.
   Summary: A primary level introduction to farming—
its history, kinds of farms, methods and machinery, and
what farmers do.
   1. Agriculture—Juvenile literature. [Agriculture.
2. Farms] I. Title.
S519.F7 1983   630   83-15010
ISBN 0-516-01693-8   AACR2

TABLE OF CONTENTS

A field of corn

A SHORT HISTORY OF FARMING

People first appeared on earth over a million years ago. Early people obtained food by hunting and gathering. They ate such plant foods as nuts, berries, and seeds. They hunted animals for meat.

The hunters and gatherers didn't have permanent homes. Once they had eaten the food in one place, they moved on in search of more.

About ten thousand years ago people found an easier way to get food. They planted some seeds. The seeds grew into wheat and other food crops. They tamed animals, which gave them milk and meat. People had discovered *farming*—the raising of crops and animals.

Farming brought a whole new way of life. People no longer had to move about in search of food. They

Barn and silos in a winter sunset

built homes where they
farmed. In places where
the soil was very fertile
(rich), many people settled.
The world's first cities
grew near these farming
settlements.

The first farmers—like those of today—had one main goal. They wanted to grow as much food as possible. Early farmers began to think up ways to do this.

The soil must be tilled (loosened) for seeds to grow well in it. At first farmers tilled the soil with sticks and rocks. That took a lot of time. Then about eight thousand years ago, farmers built something that could till the land quickly. This was the plow. Early plows were made of wood and pulled by human beings.

A better plow was invented by farmers in Egypt and Mesopotamia five thousand years ago. It was pulled by oxen.

Oxen pulling a plow in Palestine, 1892

About the time that the ox-pulled plow was invented, farmers found an answer to another problem. Some places get too little rain for crops to grow. In such places, farmers dug ditches from their land to rivers. The river water flowed through the ditches

In Egypt a man-and-ox-powered waterwheel pumps water to irrigate the crops.

Modern irrigation systems

to the thirsty crops.
Bringing water to dry land
is called irrigation. By a
thousand years ago people
had built irrigation systems
in Egypt, China, South
America, and in what is
now the United States.

An early steam-driven tractor

In the ten-thousand-year history of farming, the biggest changes have come in the last few hundred years. In the 1700s, the machine age began. Many machines have been invented to help

Left: Attaching the cups of an
electric milking machine
Above: A modern tractor

farmers. The steel plow
and the tractor are just
two of them.

Electric machinery has
made farm work easier. On
modern farms electric
machines milk cows and
do much of the work that
people once had to do.

13

Two farmers in Yugoslavia bring their cow in from the fields for the night.

In India a woman spreads grain to dry in the sun.

TWO KINDS
OF FARMING

Many of the world's
farmers plant crops and
raise livestock for one
purpose—to feed their
families. They get milk
from their cow or goat.
Eggs come from their
chickens. They eat
potatoes, corn, or whatever
crops they grow. If they
don't have other animals,
they may never eat meat.

People who live on the foods they produce are said to do subsistence farming. Subsistence farmers raise barely enough food to feed their families. There are millions of subsistence farmers. Most *can't* grow enough food to feed their families.

Life is hard for subsistence farmers. Too much or too little rain can ruin their crops. Disease can kill crops and animals.

Even today, some farmers still use animal-drawn plows.

Then thousands of people may starve.

These farmers can't buy machines. They till their fields with animal-drawn plows, much like their ancestors of long ago. They plant their seeds by hand. The entire family works in the field to harvest the crop by hand.

There are millions of subsistence farmers in Central America, South America, Africa, and Asia.

In the United States and other wealthy nations, few farmers depend only on what they produce for food. These farmers grow crops or raise livestock to sell. Farmers who sell their products are said to do commercial farming.

Left: Dairy cattle
Above: Soybean field

KINDS OF COMMERCIAL FARMS

There are different kinds of commercial farms. Crop farms grow corn, beans, cotton, and other crops. Dairy farms raise milk

19

Left: Beef cattle in winter
Above: Chickens on a poultry farm

cows. On poultry farms birds, especially chickens, are raised for their eggs and meat.

Ranching is a special kind of farming. On ranches animals, especially beef cattle and sheep, are raised. Ranch workers are usually called ranchers rather than farmers.

DECIDING WHAT TO GROW OR RAISE

How do farmers decide what to grow or raise? First they must know the climate in their area. Some plants need a warm climate. Others grow well where it is cool. Still others need lots of rain. Oranges and grapefruit, for example, need warmth.

Harvesting wheat

A close-up of wheat

Because of Florida's climate, many of its farmers grow oranges and grapefruit.

The type of soil also helps the farmer decide what to grow. Each crop grows best in a certain kind of soil. Wheat needs soil that has a lot of humus (decayed animals or plants). Much of Russia and the United States has such soil. They are the two top wheat-growing nations.

Black Angus beef cattle

Livestock graze on grasses. Farmers who own large amounts of grasslands often decide to raise livestock. Texas and Argentina have the rich grasslands beef cattle need. Both places raise beef cattle.

WHAT FARMERS DO

Farmers who raise crops work hard. They plow the soil. They use fertilizer to make the soil better and to help the plants grow. They use chemicals to kill weeds, control plant diseases, and kill insects.

Farmers make sure that their crops get enough water. If rainfall is light, they use sprinklers or other means of irrigation.

When the crops are ready, farmers harvest (pick) them. Once harvested, the crops are taken to market. There they are sold.

Ranchers must see to it that their livestock are fed and healthy. They shelter the animals from cold weather. They make sure that the births of baby animals go smoothly.

Left: A tractor pulls this 24-row planter
Above: Tractor loading a manure spreader

FARM MACHINERY

In wealthy countries, machines help farmers do their work.

On most modern farms, plows and other machines are pulled by tractors. The farmer drives the tractor like a car—only much slower.

Seed drills plant the seeds for farmers. First the drill makes holes in the ground. Then it drops the seeds into the holes.

The combine is an important farm machine. It harvests wheat and other crops. It also threshes grain crops (picks out the grain kernels from the rest of the plant).

Hooking up a tractor to a seed drill

A combine at work in a soybean field

Farmers use machines to pick pineapples, cherries, alfalfa, and many other crops. Harvesting machines save farmers time. A mechanical cherry picker can do the work of a hundred human pickers.

Modern ranches also have many machines. They are used to keep young animals warm, feed livestock, and do many other jobs.

MODERN
FARMING METHODS

Farming today is a science. Modern farmers use many methods that were unknown in past years.

Contour plowing is an important farming method.

This wheat field is an example of contour plowing.

Top: Contour plowing
Below: Tomato harvest
Below right: A cabbage field

It involves plowing across, rather than up, slopes. With this method, farm fields better conserve (retain) rainfall.

Crop rotation is also important. If the same crop is planted on the same land every year, it can use up important minerals. Farmers who rotate their crops plant different crops from year to year. They plant crops that replace minerals used up by previous crops.

Wind-eroded soil (above) contrasts sharply with fertile farmland (below).

In many places of the world, dust storms have eroded (blown away) soil. To avoid soil erosion, many farmers plant cover crops. These are crops, such as alfalfa, that help hold down the soil.

Planting rice in Thailand

Farmers and scientists have bred many new and improved plant seeds. In the 1960s, a new type of rice seed was bred. It produces bigger harvests than the rice seeds of the past. This is very important, because more than two billion people eat rice as their main food.

The careful breeding of livestock has helped ranchers. The new breeds of cattle give more beef and milk than those of years past.

Some farmers dust their crops to prevent diseases and pests.

Haying on an Amish farm

FARMERS STUDY ALL THEIR LIVES

Many people who want to be farmers go to agricultural colleges. There they learn about soil and crops. They also learn about animals. They learn how to be good farmers.

Farmers never stop learning. Their business is always changing. New seeds are bred. Better

A pineapple harvest in Puerto Rico

farm machinery is built.
Farmers must keep track
of these changes.

Farmers must study the
weather all their lives, too.
A dry period means that
they may have to irrigate.

Farmers also keep
careful track of prices.

They must know how much they can expect to earn for their crops. If a crop isn't making money, they may have to switch to a different one.

Left: Onion field
Below: Tobacco field and drying shed

A farmers market in Vanatu, an island country in the Southwest Pacific

THE FUTURE OF FARMING

Hunger is one of the great problems facing human beings. At this moment many millions of the world's people are hungry. Each year thousands of people die because they don't get enough to eat. Most of the hungry people live in countries that don't or can't grow enough food to feed them.

The United Nations and the governments of many countries are trying to help these hungry people. They are teaching poor farmers how to prepare the land so that their crops will grow better. They are teaching them about seeds that will grow bigger and better crops.

It is important for farmers in the poorer

nations to learn better
farming methods. Then one
of the main problems
facing human beings—the
problem of hunger—may
one day be conquered.

WORDS YOU SHOULD KNOW

agriculture(AG • rih • kul • cher)—farming

breeding(BREE • ding)—the production of new kinds of plants or animals by carefully choosing their parents

climate(KLY • mit)—the kind of weather an area usually has

combine(CAHM • byne)—a farm machine that harvests and threshes wheat and other crops

commercial farming(kuh • MER • shil FAR • ming)—farming done to make money

conservation(kahn • ser • VAY • shun)—the protection of soil, water, and other aspects of the environment

conserve(kun • SERVE)—to keep or protect

contour plowing(KAHN • toor)—a kind of plowing done across, rather than up, slopes. It is done to conserve moisture from rainfall

cover crops(KUH • ver CROPZ)—crops planted to help hold down the soil

crop rotation(KROP roh • TAY • shun)—the planting of different crops from year to year to replace lost minerals in the soil

dairy farm(DARE • ee FARM)—a farm that produces milk

farming(FAR • ming)—the raising of crops and livestock

fertile(FUR • til)—rich

humus(HYOO • mus)—decayed animals or plants

hunters and gatherers—ancient people who traveled about hunting and gathering their food instead of producing it themselves

irrigation(ear • ih • GAY • shun)—the process of bringing water to dry land

livestock(LYVE • stahk)—farm animals that produce food

market(MAR • kit)—the place where farm goods are sold

organic farming(or • GAN • ik) — farming in which natural substances, rather than man-made chemicals, are used to combat pests and fertilize the land

plow(PLOW) — a tool used to loosen the soil

poultry(POLE • tree) — birds that provide eggs and meat

ranching(RAN • ching) — the raising of animals, especially beef cattle and sheep, on big farms

seed drill(SEED DRILL) — a machine that plants seeds

soil erosion(SOYLE eh • ROH • jun) — the wearing or blowing away of the soil

subsistence farming(sub • SIS • tence) — a kind of farming in which people at best barely produce enough food to support themselves

thresh(THRESH) — to pick out the grain kernels from the rest of a plant

till(TILL) — to plow the soil

tractor(TRAK • ter) — a machine that pulls farm equipment

INDEX

About the Author

Dennis Fradin attended Northwestern University on a partial creative writing scholarship and graduated in 1967. He has published stories and articles in such places as Ingenue, The Saturday Evening Post, Scholastic, Chicago, *and* National Humane Review. *His previous books include the* Young People's Stories of Our States *series for Childrens Press and* Bad Luck Tony *for Prentice-Hall. He is married and the father of three children.*